EVERMORE
from BEAUTY AND THE BEAST

Music by ALAN MENKEN
Lyrics by TIM RICE

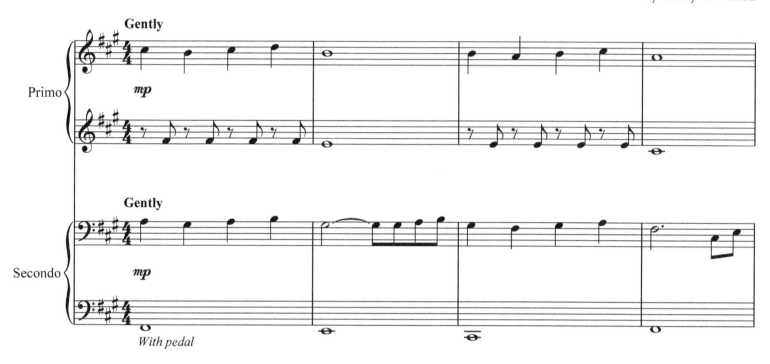

© 2017 Wonderland Music Company, Inc.
All Rights Reserved. Used by Permission.

2ND EDITION

CONTEMPORARY
Disney DUETS

ISBN 978-1-5400-3873-9

Disney characters and artwork © Disney

Walt Disney Music Company
Wonderland Music Company, Inc.

HAL•LEONARD®

For all works contained herein:
Unauthorized copying, arranging, adapting, recording, Internet posting, public performance,
or other distribution of the music in this publication is an infringement of copyright.
Infringers are liable under the law.

Visit Hal Leonard Online at
www.halleonard.com

Contact us:
Hal Leonard
7777 West Bluemound Road
Milwaukee, WI 53213
Email: info@halleonard.com

In Europe, contact:
Hal Leonard Europe Limited
42 Wigmore Street
Marylebone, London, W1U 2RN
Email: info@halleonardeurope.com

In Australia, contact:
Hal Leonard Australia Pty. Ltd.
4 Lentara Court
Cheltenham, Victoria, 3192 Australia
Email: info@halleonard.com.au

HOW DOES A MOMENT LAST FOREVER

from BEAUTY AND THE BEAST

Music by ALAN MENKEN
Lyrics by TIM RICE

© 2017 Wonderland Music Company, Inc.
All Rights Reserved. Used by Permission.

HOW FAR I'LL GO
from MOANA

Music and Lyrics by
LIN-MANUEL MIRANDA

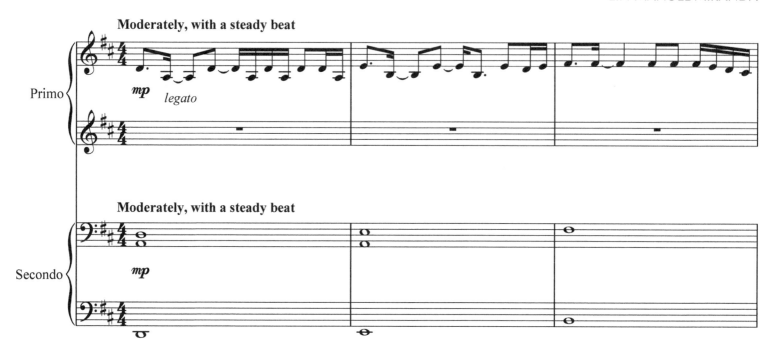

© 2016 Walt Disney Music Company
All Rights Reserved. Used by Permission.

LAVA
from LAVA

Music and Lyrics by
JAMES FORD MURPHY

© 2015 Walt Disney Music Company and Pixar Talking Pictures
All Rights Reserved. Used by Permission.

LET IT GO
from FROZEN

Music and Lyrics by KRISTEN ANDERSON-LOPEZ
and ROBERT LOPEZ

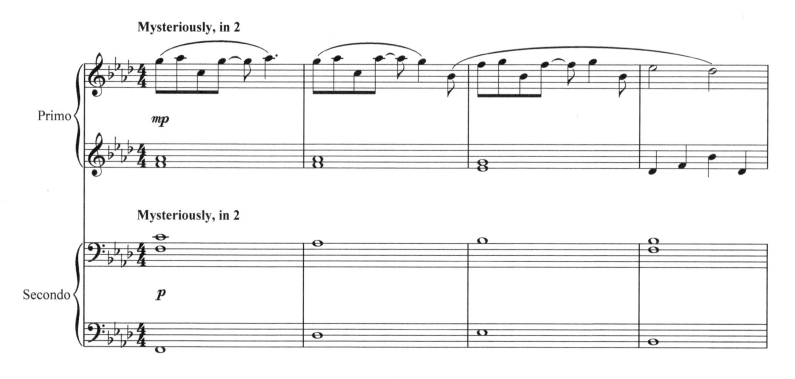

© 2013 Wonderland Music Company, Inc.
All Rights Reserved. Used by Permission

REMEMBER ME
(Ernesto de la Cruz)
from COCO

Words and Music by KRISTEN ANDERSON-LOPEZ
and ROBERT LOPEZ

© 2017 Wonderland Music Company, Inc. and Pixar Music
All Rights Reserved. Used by Permission.

YOU'RE WELCOME

from MOANA

Music and Lyrics by
LIN-MANUEL MIRANDA

© 2016 Walt Disney Music Company
All Rights Reserved. Used by Permission.

PROUD CORAZÓN
from COCO

Music by GERMAINE FRANCO
Lyrics by ADRIAN MOLINA

© 2017 Walt Disney Music Company and Pixar Talking Pictures
All Rights Reserved. Used by Permission.